# Witness
to Our
Times

———

# Witness to Our Times

## My Life as a Photojournalist

### Flip Schulke

in association with Matt Schudel

Cricket Books

*A Marcato Book*

Chicago

## Acknowledgments

A word/photography book of one's life's work could not be done without the gifts of time, creativity, and mentoring of a great many persons. Time and memory dim the names of all those whose contributions led to my career's output. Please forgive any names omitted herein.

## Collaborator

My deepest thanks to my collaborator, Matt Schudel, who has the ability to take my outpouring of verbalizations and turn them into easily understandable prose. He is both friend and coworker.

## My Family

Thanks to Donna Schulke, Robin and Stuart Seymour, Paul and Lynn Schulke and their children Kyle and Sara, Lisa and Don Davidson and their children Jackie and Catey, Maria and Allen Cohen and their children Leighton and Sterling, and to my stepson Joe Toreno and his partner, Amanda Friedman.

Thanks to stepson John Toreno—who is my greatest P.R. man and general all-around promotions manager—and to my older sister, Roxy, and her husband, John Kaufmann, who have given much encouragement all along.

## Workers

Special thanks to Gary Truman, manager of FS Archives; his wife, Grace; and my assistant, Jesse Palmer. A photographer's work is only as good as those who end up handling the photographic prints: at Thomson Photo Imaging, Miami, Florida, Howard Thomson (retired), Skip Thomson, Edith Cromeyer, Joe Lucinian, Paul Plyer, Andrea Maitland, Kip Cowan, and Beltran Expinosa; at Modernage Photographic Services, New York, New York, Ricki Troiano, Kenneth Troiano, Richard Troiano, Wolfram Kloetz, Jorge Fiqueroa, and Vernon Sege; at Sammy's Camera, Los Angeles, California, Karla Walters, professional sales manager.

## Along the Way

My heartfelt appreciation to the late Howard Chapnick, Jeanette Chapnick, and Ben Chapnick at Black Star Agency; to James Danziger and Phil Kunhardt at *Life* magazine; and to Mike Durham, Ed Reingold, Bob Fellows, Wayne Warga, Don Underwood, Mike Silva, Miguel Acoca, Dick Billings, and Hank Suydam, all writers with *Life* who accompanied me on so many assignments.

Thanks to Bill Lyons of UPI and Jim Boudier of AP, with whom I traded film and "secret" information, unbeknownst to all of our publications. I will always treasure the closeness and friendships between all of the Southern photographers covering civil rights events. Special thanks to Don Carlton and the Center for American History, University of Texas, who gave a permanent home to my archive of 600,000 original negatives, color slides, and prints, along with 9,000 selected digitized photographs. Thanks also to Macalester College, St. Paul, Minnesota, for accepting the digitized photographs, to be used by the student body. Thanks to Ros, Andrew, and Matthew Duggan in Basingstoke, UK; and Madeleine and Catherine Andre-Montenay, in Tours, France.

Thanks to Jennifer Podis, staff photographer at the *Palm Beach Post*.

I am extremely grateful to my literary agent, Jennifer Lyons, who has placed my books with very fine publishers.

My hat is off to Marc Aronson, publisher of Cricket Books, whose idea it was to do this book on my professional life. A special heartfelt thanks to Carol Saller, an editor who understands the use of words and pictures together, and to Tony Jacobson, art director, who is truly talented in combining words and pictures on the printed page. He made the book sparkle.

## Finis

As I said in this book, my life is a sum of my heritage; my hometown, New Ulm, Minnesota; Macalester College, with all of its wonderful teachers who took a personal interest in my learning; and the University of Miami and the University of Missouri/Columbia, where I taught. My deepest regards to all the photographers who have preceded me and to my peers, who have silently influenced my life's work and my life's love: photography, communicating with people about the world around me.

Library of Congress Cataloging-in-Publication Data

Schulke, Flip.
  Witness to our times : my life as a photojournalist / Flip Schulke,
with Matt Schudel.
     p. cm.
Summary: An autobiography of a man whose documentary photographs in American magazines helped to shape public opinion on such issues as the civil rights movement and the space race.
Includes bibliographical references and index.
  ISBN 0-8126-2682-6 (Cloth : alk. paper)
  1. Schulke, Flip—Juvenile literature. 2. News photographers—United States—Biography—Juvenile literature. 3. Documentary photography—United States—Juvenile literature. [1. Schulke, Flip. 2. Photographers. 3. Documentary photography.] I. Schudel, Matt. II. Title.
  TR140.S39 A3 2002
  070.4'9'092--dc21

                                                    2002151457

*Definition. "Muse: the spirit regarded as inspiring those practicing liberal arts."*

*My wife, Donna Lee Schulke, is the muse who has inspired and motivated me to embark on the recounting of my life's work and its experiences. Without her, the following work would never have been written.*

———————————————

*In memory of Father James Keller, MM, founder, in 1945, of the Christophers, an informal organization teaching that each individual, molded in the divine image, is given a special task in life, which belongs to no one else. This is summed up by the ancient Chinese proverb "It is better to light one candle than to curse the darkness."*

*Because of these teachings, I entered into the profession of photo-journalism.*

# Contents

# Prologue

*"I was a gymnast in high school—that's how I got my name, 'Flip'—*
*and a buddy of mine put a trampoline on the back of a truck for the*
*local town parade. He wanted some pictures of himself,*
*but neither one of us had a camera, so I went*
*down to the drugstore and bought a Kodak*
*Brownie Special for $4. This was in 1947.*

*"I took the film in to get it processed,*
*looked at the pictures, and thought, Gee,*
*these are pretty good. I started to shoot*
*family pictures, sold the reprints, and ended*
*up making some good money.*

*"In high school, I visited a newsroom and*
*an industrial photography studio. From seeing*
*the excitement of the newsroom and going into the*
*darkroom, I knew that's what I wanted to do. I have*
*supported myself from the age of 15 on as a photographer.*

Flip, far left in front row, with the gymnastics team at New Ulm (Minnesota) High School, 1948

"After I graduated from Macalester College in my home state of Minnesota, I moved to Miami, which turned out to be a great place to develop a career as a photojournalist. I never cared about just taking pretty pictures. I've always thought of myself as a reporter.

"In 1958, I met Martin Luther King, Jr., in Miami, and we hit it off right away. I could see that the South was going to be the battle ground of the growing civil rights movement, and King helped put me inside the movement, which is probably what I'm best known for.

"I made my living as a freelance photojournalist and I had to be ready for anything. I shot football games, car races, profiles of small towns, Fidel Castro and the Cuban revolution, Elvis Presley, Muhammad Ali, John F. Kennedy, popes, astronauts, the Berlin Wall, TV stars, you name it. Florida was a good place for scuba diving, and I developed a specialty in underwater photography. I traveled all over the world, shooting for Life, National Geographic, and European magazines and newspapers. If I had to guess, I'd estimate that I've shot about 500,000 images in my career.

"The 1960s were kind of a golden age for photojournalism. It was an exciting time in history. Some people say the '60s destroyed America. But the '60s are what made America.

*Woman in pharmacy, Lanzarote, Canary Islands, 1968*

*Mickey Mantle signing autograph for Flip's son, Paul, 1965*

"I also spent a lot of time in Europe and I was there just after the Berlin Wall went up. Later on, I went back when the Wall came down in 1989, marking the beginning of the fall of communism.

"My pictures might be important to history, but I have never considered myself a player in history. I'm a recorder of what's going on. Except with Dr. King, I tried not to get close to the people I worked with, because I wanted to show them as they were. I didn't want them acting for me.

"I'm an idealist when it comes to journalism. I'm an advocate and have always been an advocate. But I'm also fair. My hope all along has been that what I was photographing might influence people to try to do better for themselves and for the world."

*Future president Dwight D. Eisenhower campaigning in Minnesota, 1952*

*From the world gymnastics championships in Prague, Czechoslovakia (now the Czech Republic), 1962*

*Football great Johnny Unitas, Baltimore, 1964.*

*Television star Jackie Gleason during a live performance of his show in Miami Beach, 1962*

# Introduction

Flip Schulke's decade-long friendship with Martin Luther King, Jr., put him on the front lines of the civil rights revolution of the 1950s and '60s, and his work in *Life* magazine made him one of America's preeminent photojournalists. Flip was in Washington in 1963, when King made his stirring "I have a dream" speech. He traveled the back roads of Alabama, Mississippi, Louisiana, and Georgia, using his camera to bear witness to the greatest movement for social change in the twentieth century. He captured the mood of the time in faces filled with rage, fear, hope, and, all too often, grief.

Flip had never known anyone like King—a dramatic, eloquent speaker whose moral authority made the nation realize that black Americans had been denied the same rights that had long been granted to white citizens.

In the winter and early spring of 1965, the forces of change met the forces of resistance in the small Alabama city of Selma. When King tried to register at Selma's previously segregated Hotel Albert, he was punched in the face and kicked in the groin by a white supremacist.

*Selma, Alabama, 1965*

During protest marches in Selma over a period of two months, more than 2,000 people, including schoolchildren, were arrested. Rogue cops sometimes attacked the marchers with tear gas, whips, clubs, and cattle prods. A white Unitarian minister was beaten to death.

"King always taught his people to practice nonviolence," says Flip. "It's what gave the civil rights movement its moral force. But in Selma, the threat of physical attack became an ugly reality."

In more than a decade as a photojournalist, Flip had learned to keep his mouth shut and let his camera do his talking.

"As a journalist, my job was to observe the news, not to participate in it. I had always stayed away from participating in events because it was my job to record what was going on around me."

But that day in Selma, when he saw police and vigilantes attacking innocent children, he could no longer stand by.

"It's hard for me to talk about some of these things; I get all choked up," he says, years later. "These kids were hurting. Anyway, I pushed a club away from a policeman. The whole thing lasted maybe 45 seconds.

"It was the first time I had ever gotten involved in a story I was supposed to be covering. Afterward, King pulled me aside and said, 'Flip, you did wrong. I can understand your losing your temper, but unless you record what happened, the world won't know that child got beaten. We as a people have been beaten and murdered for a couple of hundred years. Your role is to photograph what is happening to us. You can't be a participant.'

"I was embarrassed that I hadn't thought of it that way. I think that was a real watershed mark in my whole understanding of what I was trying to do with my life in journalism.

"I first became interested in journalism because I saw it as a way to make a difference in the world. But in all the years I had been working, no one had so clearly spelled out the difference between observing

*Flip after being tear-gassed at Canton, Mississippi, 1966. Photo by Robert J. Ellison.*

history and being a participant. The important thing was to illustrate what you saw happening so that people would understand better by seeing your pictures."

# CHAPTER 1

# Early Years

Flip Schulke was born in St. Paul, Minnesota, on June 24, 1930. His family was well-off, especially for the time, less than a year after the stock market crash plunged the entire nation into a depression. In 1918, his grandfather had opened Schulke's department store in the small city of New Ulm, which made the family prosper.

Flip, whose given name was Graeme Phelps Schulke, grew up as a member of the Episcopal church and did not learn until much later that his mother was half Jewish. Flip's father, who embraced many of the unsavory prejudices of his time, detested both African Americans and Jews and was not shy about sharing his opinions. He was ashamed of his wife's Jewish heritage and claimed her maiden name was Coleman when it was really Kalman. He often reprimanded

Flip for his behavior, including gesturing when he spoke, claiming it was "a Jewish trait."

The Schulke family spent winters in Miami and, later, in the exclusive Florida resort town of Palm Beach. At the time, Florida was a much more traditionally Southern state than it is today, and a number of African Americans worked in the family home.

*"Our black cook became a surrogate mother to me. Black people were not only in the house, but they brought their children. I always found it easy to get along with them. I learned at a very early age that you judge somebody not on their color or their religion, but on who they are."*

In 1944, after Flip's father had failed to pay his income taxes for several years, the Internal Revenue Service caught up with him. As the family's fortunes took a sudden turn for the worse, the Schulkes spent the cold winter of 1945 at their house in New Hampshire, where Flip stoked the furnace at night and tried to stay away from his father's increasingly frequent drunken outbursts.

*"I never did anything right in his eyes. I caught my father in so many lies. He lied about everything, and I always took the opposite side. I was stubborn and I believed that truth was truth. The guy was just an ogre to me. He was a violent disciplinarian and would use his belt on me. It reached a point where I couldn't take it any longer."*

In February 1946, when Flip was 15, he took $300 from his father's wallet and left home for good. He rode a train back to New Ulm, a town of 15,000 populated mostly by the descendants of German immigrants. After his privileged childhood, Flip found himself shining shoes to earn money. He moved in with the family of the football coach and, after missing a full year of school, enrolled at New Ulm High School. His great-uncle on his mother's side supported Flip with a monthly allowance of

$25, but he also encouraged Flip to work on his own as a dishwasher and cook.

*"My great-uncle let me live a worker's life, which was the greatest thing he could have done. I had to earn my own living. I made a lot of friends and was accepted in the town because I had done everything on my own."*

It was in high school that Flip began to take pictures with his first camera, a two-and-a-half-inch-square "Baby Brownie." Starting with the town parade, he went on to photograph his fellow high-school students and to take family portraits. Eventually, he made enough money to buy a Speed Graphic camera and a 1932 Plymouth, making him the only student in his high school with his own car.

*Flip at the wheel of his 1932 Plymouth, with high-school friends, 1949*

*"Every girl in the school wanted a picture of her hero on the football field. The New Ulm Daily Journal would buy pictures of school games from me. As a senior in high school, I was picture editor of the yearbook.*

*"The St. Paul Pioneer Press had a weekly photo competition. I took a photo of an old German guy with a pipe, sent it in, and won $5. I was beginning to look around New Ulm and document it.*

*"I didn't get into photography from any deep feelings to communicate with the world—my interest in working as a journalist came as I went along. My first reason for getting into photography was to make money."*

1950

In the fall of 1949, Flip enrolled at Macalester College in St. Paul. He had joined the National Guard while still in high school, and when the United States entered the Korean War in 1950, he and his new wife, Marlene, were sent to an army base in Alabama, where Flip was a young sergeant in charge of a darkroom. Their oldest daughter, Robin, was born on the base. After nine months, Flip's hitch was up, and he went back to Minnesota, having missed only one semester of college.

*"My main influence at Macalester was Ivan Burg, who had been picture editor at the St. Paul Pioneer Press. Ivan said a good reporter is supposed to keep his eyes open. He took the rules of journalism and put them into picture journalism. A photojournalist has to find picture stories—this was*

*a new idea. By my sophomore year, I knew that's what I wanted to do."*

At Macalester, Flip had a triple major in political science, sociology, and journalism and even found time to be on the college swimming team. He studied religion, philosophy, and history and also took a course on race relations, which brought to mind some of the warm experiences with the black people he had met in Florida in his youth. As a convert to Catholicism, he was also strongly affected by the teachings of a religious group called the Christophers, who believed that artists, journalists, and politicians had a responsibility to use their talents to make the world a better place.

*Minnesota State Fair, 1951*

*"I saw the unfair way blacks were being treated and I couldn't stand the intolerance. I believed in America. We had just gone through the Second World War, when we were fighting for freedom, freedom for all people. I was very influenced by Lewis Hine, who did photographs of child labor. I wanted to be like the writers who exposed injustice."*

When he was a junior at Macalester in 1952, Flip was named College Photographer of the Year. As part of his award, he attended a workshop at the University of Missouri, where he learned about photo agencies—syndicates that hire photographers and sell their work to publications around the world. He saw Black Star on a list of agencies and liked the name.

*"I got back to college and wrote to Black Star, asking how I could get connected with them. They sent me a polite kiss-off letter, only I was so naive I didn't know what it was. It was very encouraging, saying my work was good and that I should keep in touch. To me, this was the voice of God, so I kept sending them story ideas.*

*"I had learned all along from everyone that you get ahead by selling ideas. There are plenty of good photographers, but the ones who rise above are the ones who come up with ideas the editors don't know about.*

*"One of my ideas was about my German American hometown. Black Star gave me my first paying assignment, for the U.S. Information Agency, and told me I should spend a couple of days there. They didn't need the pictures for two months, so I spent eight weekends in New Ulm, covering every angle of the town. I shot 20 rolls of film. When I sent them in, my editor said anybody who would work that hard could learn to be a good photographer."*

# CHAPTER 2

# "The Divine Seed of Discontent"

In January 1954, after graduating from Macalester, Flip moved to Florida, where he had been offered a job as a staff photographer and part-time instructor at the University of Miami. One of the people he met in Miami was a retiree named Wilson Hicks, who was an unofficial advisor to the university's student publications. For nearly 20 years, Hicks had been the picture editor and executive editor of *Life* magazine. While he was there, he created the photography department that became renowned for publishing the finest photojournalism in the world. After they met on campus, Hicks asked Flip to show him his work.

*"When I left his house that night at 4 A.M., I thought he was the greatest person I had ever met. He was the first person who understood what I was trying to do with picture stories and photojournalism. I wanted to do what those guys who worked for him at Life did.*

*Flip photographing noted Life magazine photographer W. Eugene Smith at a photojournalism conference at the University of Miami, 1959.*

"I became his protégé. I'd go to him every week, and we would go through my work page by page. He said, 'I hope you don't expect me to say your pictures are nice. You will learn something only if I can criticize. I will always tell you how something could be done differently.' He said it was important to know the past, in photography, so you won't take the obvious path.

"He also told me something when I first met him that I'll never forget: 'What you need is a little sprinkling of the divine seed of discontent.' In other words, you should always be a little dissatisfied with what you do. You shouldn't feel that you've reached the pinnacle and don't need to learn any more. A divine seed of discontent makes you just a little bit apprehensive that you don't know it all.

*"To me, Wilson Hicks was a great man because I was nothing compared with the people he had been working with. I have the same feeling of responsibility toward young photographers today."*

Through Hicks, Flip became friends with two of the most storied photographers of *Life*—W. Eugene Smith and Margaret Bourke-White, whose photograph of the Fort Peck Dam had been on the cover of the very first issue of *Life* in 1936. Flip wanted nothing more than to join their ranks, but when he was given his first assignment for *Life*—about a stripper—he turned it down because he knew his wife would object.

The same year that Flip moved to Miami, 1954, a new magazine named *Sports Illustrated* was founded, and Flip's work began to appear in the fledgling weekly and in other magazines, including *National*

*Flip with color photography pioneer Ernst Haas, 1957. Haas was instrumental in helping Flip land his first major assignment with National Geographic. Photo © Ray Fisher.*

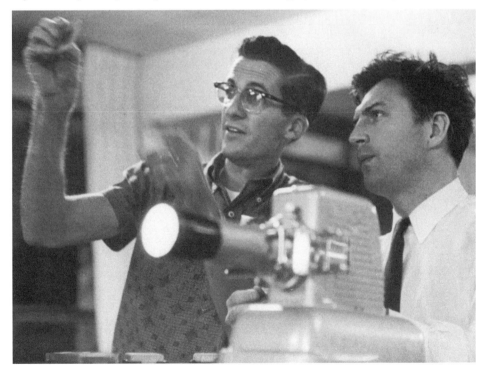

*In 1956, Flip spent a month photographing people in the mountain town of Burnsville, North Carolina, for National Geographic, his first major picture story in a national magazine.*

*Geographic*. At the same time, he was developing a specialty that would become an important part of his career. As a boy, Flip once made a diving mask out of the glass face of a clock and a rubber inner tube from a tire, and in college he had been a member of the swimming team. He learned scuba diving in Miami and began to experiment with taking pictures under water. He invented a domed lens system that eliminated optical distortion under water.

Flip was planning to photograph a popular Florida water-skiing attraction when Hicks, his mentor, idly asked what water-skiing would look like

*Some of the pioneering camera housings and lens systems that Flip developed for underwater photography*

*Flip in wet suit, late 1960s*

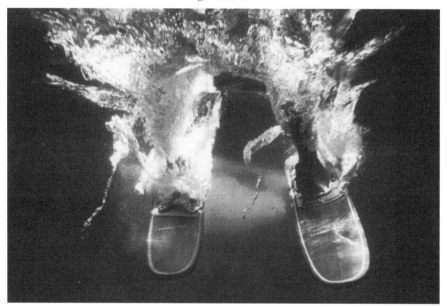

*Underwater photographs of water-skiing, from Flip's first photographic essay in Life magazine, 1959*

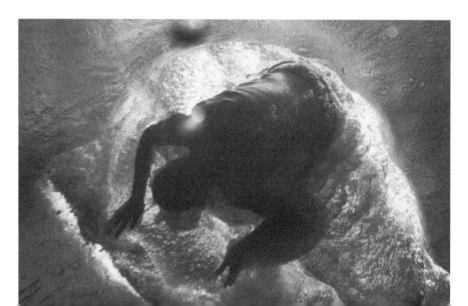

from under water. As a result, Flip ended up with his first photo essay in *Life,* on July 13, 1959, and won a prize for sports photography.

After his work began to appear regularly in the pages of the nation's most prestigious publications, Flip was offered staff positions with both *National Geographic* and *Life*. He turned down the opportunities in order to be a freelance photographer. He worked under a series of independent contracts for *Life* and, at the same time, continued to sell his work through the Black Star agency.

Flip traveled widely throughout the South and the Caribbean. He was in Havana in January 1959 when Fidel Castro seized control of Cuba. At the time, Castro was not seen as a future dictator but as a youthful revolutionary with a gift for florid phrases. As Flip waited through a three-hour speech in Havana one night, camera at the ready, he managed to capture the precise moment when a white dove landed on Castro's shoulder.

*Cuban revolutionary leader Fidel Castro, shortly after seizing power in Havana, January 1959*

*"That was partly luck and partly preparation. I had done my home-work and talked to the people on the street and found out where Castro would be speaking that night—no one else knew ahead of time. I saw a farmer who had a crate full of doves and I watched to see when he'd release them."*

Back in the United States the following year, a very different kind of young revolutionary, Elvis Presley, was returning to civilian life after two years in the army. One of his first performances was to be in Miami Beach. Even though photographs weren't supposed to be allowed, Flip went to the rehearsal anyway. The lighting crew at the theater let him climb into the framework above the stage, where he got a series of bird's-eye shots of Elvis from above.

*Elvis Presley in Miami Beach, 1960*

*Actor Robert Vaughn in costume for* The Bridge at Remagen, *filmed in Czechoslovakia, 1968*

A year later, in 1961, Flip met a 19-year-old athlete who was unknown to the general public but would become one of the most recognizable figures in the world—the boxer later known as Muhammad Ali.

*"When Sports Illustrated assigned me a story about a young boxer, Cassius Clay, I had never heard of him. I showed him my underwater pictures of water-skiing to impress him that I had done a story for Life.*

"I went to the motel where he was staying, and there he was in the swimming pool going through his workout. He was doing a hook and a jab, and I could see the bubbles. I said to him, 'That's fantastic because I see your fists going through the water, like my water-skiing pictures.'

"And he said to me, right back, 'Oh, I've always done this. An old trainer up in Louisville told me that if I practice in the pool, the water resistance acts just like a weight.' It all sounded plausible to me.

"When I called the editor at Sports Illustrated, he thought I was crazy for taking pictures of a boxer in a swimming pool. So I called Life magazine, and they liked the idea. In those days, Life loved to beat out its sister publication on a story, so I went back the next day to take pictures in the pool.

"I had to wear a pair of his boxing shorts because I had forgotten my swimming trunks that day. I put on my scuba gear and got several shots of him practicing different punches in the water. Then I turned around, and there he was, standing on the bottom of the pool. I mean, that's very hard to do, and he's in a perfect boxing pose. So I swam over real quick and I got about six pictures of him. He was holding his breath all this time and not making any movement. The only regret I have is, when Life ran the story, they didn't select that picture. More people have requested that picture worldwide than any single picture I ever shot.

"Three years later, after Cassius Clay won the heavyweight championship and changed his name to Muhammad Ali, I went back to photograph him again. We were looking through a scrapbook, and when he came across my underwater pictures he winked at me. I realized he had taken me. I learned later he and his trainer had come up with the whole story on their own. He didn't even know how to swim. He fooled me, he fooled a Life reporter, he fooled everybody—and it made fantastic pictures. It showed me what a brilliant guy he was, even at 19. He thought up an idea that I would swallow. But I'm really proud of the whole thing."

CHAPTER 3

# "The Hardest Pictures I Ever Took"

When Flip met him in Miami in 1958, Martin Luther King, Jr., was already a major figure in the growing civil rights movement. He had a doctorate in theology from Boston University, had led a bus boycott in Alabama, had served time in jail, and had already been on the cover of *Time* magazine. He was only 29 years old, just one year older than Flip. At their first meeting, they stayed up all night talking about theology, King's doctrine of nonviolence, and the plight of blacks in the American South.

Through King, Flip met many other leaders of the civil rights movement and began shooting for the leading black magazines of the day, *Ebony* and *Jet*. Flip's first civil rights assignment for *Life* came in 1962, when the U.S. Supreme Court ruled that the University of Mississippi could not refuse to admit James Meredith to its law school because of his race. On September 30, 1962, Meredith was escorted onto the campus by federal marshals and civil rights lawyers, only to be met by a mob of militant white townspeople, students, Ku Klux Klan members, and local police officers. Snipers shot at the federal agents and journalists.

*"The highway patrol had surrounded the entrance to the campus and prevented the press from getting in. I met a professor who lived on campus, and he told me he could get me on campus by putting me in the back of his car with a blanket over me."*

Even though he was suffering the effects of tear gas, Flip managed to get an eerie nighttime shot showing a military tank silhouetted, amid hazy smoke, against an elegant columned building on the university campus.

*"I was hiding in bushes and could hear the cracks of the rifles. I saw a French photographer running and told him to get down. 'This is nothing compared to Cyprus,' he said. A few minutes later, he was killed by a sniper.*

*Tear gas and tanks on the campus of the University of Mississippi, 1962*

*"As soon as I heard that the photographer had been killed, I realized how dangerous it was. The camera is like a wall between you and danger, and you take chances. I had never been under fire before. You wonder if it's worth it. I had four children, and they would sometimes see me in dangerous situations on television and get frightened. I reached a point where I decided that if I was going to risk my life, it had to be for something I truly, deeply believed in."*

Two people were killed in the disturbance, and 28 federal marshals received gunshot wounds. The riot lasted for 15 hours and was quelled only when President Kennedy ordered 16,000 regular army troops into action. Only then was Meredith able to attend class as the first African American student at the University of Mississippi.

Four decades after the fact, it is hard for many younger Americans to understand how dangerous it was to march for civil rights or to cover the movement as a journalist. Flip was threatened by gun-toting white supremacists and police officers, and his car was often followed.

*"In Alabama we were followed by trucks with rifles in the back windows. We were always very frightened, always. If you were really in trouble, you would stay in the black sections. We would change cars and license plates all the time. I always rented Cadillacs because they had big engines that could outrun the pickup trucks of the white mobs."*

Flip captured some of his most dramatic—and frightening—civil rights images in Alabama, after federal courts ordered the state to integrate the schools. The governor of the state, George Wallace, had vowed, "Segregation now! Segregation tomorrow! Segregation forever!" and made a defiant stance in a schoolhouse door to block integration. When federal officials accompanied black students to class in 1963, the white students poured out en masse.

*Alabama governor George Wallace in his office, September 10, 1963*

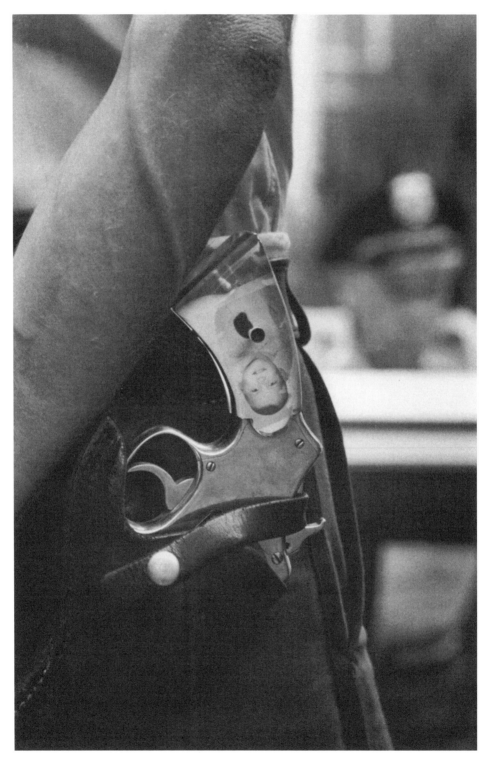

*Policeman's pistol, Montgomery, Alabama, 1963*

*"Outside the school there were segregationists with Confederate flags. They hated photographers and they did a lot to try to block us. The black kids arrived, guarded by U.S. marshals. They went into the school, and it just emptied of the white kids. That's when I got the picture of the screaming white girls.*

*"What bothered me the most was what I heard them yelling. They were screaming every dirty word in the book. At that time, you never heard words like that in public. It really affected me as a person. I hadn't realized how horribly ingrained this hatred was, for these girls to say the things they said in public. It really had to be extreme.*

*"I thought this had gone too far and I decided I wanted to do anything I could to show how widespread this hatred for blacks truly was."*

*White high-school students walked out of class and cursed black students on the first day that public schools were integrated in Montgomery, Alabama, 1963.*

*Montgomery, Alabama, 1963*

On the night of June 12, 1963, a civil rights leader named Medgar Evers was shot and killed on the front steps of his own house in Jackson, Mississippi. Flip and a *Life* reporter drove all night from Alabama, arriving at the Evers's house at 8 A.M. Flip knocked on the door and was admitted by Evers's widow, Myrlie. They had never met, yet she allowed Flip to stay with the family all day. He was the only photographer inside the house and at the funeral home two days later, when the family held a private viewing. Myrlie Evers would later write in her book *For Us, the Living:* "I turned and the *Life* photographer was there. His eyes were filled with tears. For the first time . . . the hatred I had felt for all whites was gone. It never returned."

*"I don't know what I said, but somehow, in talking to her, my face, my body language got across how terrible I felt about what had happened. I'm sure my eyes teared up."*

Myrlie Evers with her son, Van, after the assassination of her husband, Medgar, in Jackson, Mississippi, June 1963.

Left, Medgar Evers pictured on memorial program.

Flip went to the church where the funeral would be held and found out where Mrs. Evers would be sitting. He checked the windows and positioned himself so the light would reflect off her face into his camera at a 45-degree angle. He was kneeling just beyond the casket containing the slain Medgar Evers.

*"All people are affected by emotion, and I wanted the nation to see that this family had a father who had been cut down at a very young age. I wanted to show his widow's devastation. I got a picture with just one tear coming down her face. She didn't dissolve into crying, but to me that tear was even more devastating. Those pictures across the casket were the hardest pictures I ever took."*

*Myrlie Evers at her husband's memorial service,*
*June 15, 1963*

# CHAPTER 4

# "The Greatest Man I Ever Met"

From the time of their first meeting in 1958, Flip stayed in frequent touch with Martin Luther King, Jr., covering many of his speeches, marches, and church services for *Life* and for the Black Star agency. Flip grew friendly with King's family. He called the civil rights leader "Doc."

The largest event that King organized took place on August 28, 1963. More than 250,000 people came to Washington, D.C., for what has been known ever since as the March on Washington. It was the first time that whites

*Martin Luther King, Jr., preaching at Ebenezer Baptist Church, Atlanta, Georgia*

*Martin Luther King, Jr., with his son Dexter, 1964*

*Although he was a friendly, good-natured man, Martin Luther King, Jr., seldom smiled for the camera.*

and blacks marched together in large numbers, as civil rights advocates converged on the capital from every corner of the country.

*"The leader of the Pennsylvania group asked how to get to the Washington Monument. The police told him to walk down Pennsylvania Avenue, but I piped up and said there was another route that was a lot prettier. I pointed out that they could walk down the mall, in the grass, with no cars. So I had the only picture of a huge group of people marching with signs, with the Capitol in the background."*

There had been several speeches throughout the afternoon before King took the podium as the final speaker of the day. Flip found a place where he could show King flanked by American flags as he stood on the steps of the Lincoln Memorial. It was then that King delivered his "I have a dream" speech, one of the most rousing and inspiring examples of oratory in the nation's history. "I have a dream," he said, "that my four children will one day live in a nation where they will not be judged by the color of their skin but by the content of their character."

*"I knew King was going to be the last speaker, and I had been told that he would be giving an incredible speech. There are a few times when I felt what I covered was world-shaking. The most important set of photographs I have ever taken was the March on Washington where King gave his 'I have a dream' speech."*

*The climactic moment of Martin Luther King, Jr.'s, "I have a dream" speech, when he declared, "Free at last! Free at last! Thank God almighty, we are free at last!"*

*Crowd gathered at the Lincoln Memorial for King's "I have a dream" speech, August 28, 1963*

In November 1964, after he had led services at Ebenezer Baptist Church in Atlanta, King invited Flip to his house for Sunday dinner. Flip left his cameras in his car until King invited him to bring them into the house.

*"He said, 'It's not every day you learn you won the Nobel Peace Prize.' Well, he didn't have to go any further than that. I figured he obviously wanted this occasion photographed and I stayed with him the whole day. We both had four kids, and I could tell he was a good father. He spent time with each one of his kids."*

*Martin Luther King, Jr., in his office*

*Martin Luther King, Jr., at home with his daughter Yolanda*

In June 1966, Dr. King led a march to the front steps of the Neshoba County Courthouse in Philadelphia, Mississippi. It was America's own heart of darkness. Two years before, three civil rights workers, James Chaney, Andrew Goodman, and Michael Schwerner, had been murdered and then buried in the red clay of Neshoba County. Surrounded by the local police, King gave a brief eulogy, noting that no one had been tried or punished for the deaths of the slain marchers and that killers might be among them that day.

"We're right behind you," said a voice from the courthouse window.

*"We were scared to death. There were guns all around. Later on, Dr. King said, 'I just knew I'd never see the end of that day.' Rev. Ralph Abernathy, who gave the benediction that day, said it was the most frightening experience of his life. He told me, 'I never thought we would leave there alive.'"*

In 1963, King had been arrested during a protest march in Montgomery, the state capital of Alabama. He was sentenced to jail, and four years later, on October 30, 1967, he flew to Montgomery to serve his time—four days. As Flip sat next to him on the airplane, he cautioned King about being more careful. His schedule was often published, and he usually traveled alone, without a bodyguard.

*"Doc said, 'I'm only on this earth as long as God wants me to be here. I am not being careless with my life, but when the Lord wants to take me, He will.*

*"I said, 'I wish I had your faith.' I was trying to get him to be careful, but he turned it around to talk about my soul. He was more worried about my faith than about his safety. It was the last time I saw him alive."*

Flip was in New York on April 4, 1968, when he heard the news that King had been assassinated in Memphis, Tennessee. He called King's widow, Coretta, and she invited Flip to join the family at home. The picture

*Coretta Scott King, with three of her children, at the funeral of her husband, April 1968. From left, the children are Bernice, Martin, and Dexter.*

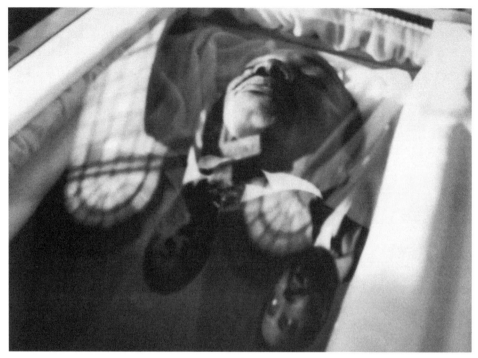

*Martin Luther King, Jr., in his casket, Ebenezer Baptist Church, Atlanta, April 1968*

*Robert F. Kennedy with Coretta King before her husband's funeral*

*Coretta King at cemetery with tearful family friend, singer Harry Belafonte*

editor of *Life* had already assigned several staff photographers to the story and told Flip he wouldn't be needed. Flip flew to Atlanta anyway. As dozens of reporters and photographers milled outside the house, only Flip got inside the door.

*"When I got to Atlanta, I called the picture editor, and he said, 'Look, I've got plenty of people already. I can't use you. Stop bothering me.'*

*"I said, 'That's nice to know because I'm calling you from inside the Martin Luther King home, and there aren't any other photographers in here.' The instant he knew where I was, all he said was, 'You're on.'*

*"*Life *had tremendous clout, and we were allowed into places that other publications and the television networks were kept out of. But none of this would have happened if I had not had this friendship."*

At the funeral, Flip could not listen to the eulogies or to any of King's taped speeches because he knew he would break down in tears. Instead, he intently watched Mrs. King through the viewfinder of his camera. He remembered the photograph he had made five years before of Myrlie Evers, as a single tear coursed down her cheek. But Mrs. King did not cry.

*"Coretta's face was totally different. I was trying to get on film what I felt her face showed. It wasn't complete sorrow; it was pride."*

Flip's picture of Coretta Scott King, sorrowful but strong under her black veil, was on the cover of *Life* magazine and was later named Picture of the Year by the National Press Photographers' Association. It has been selected as one of the 50 most memorable photographs taken since 1950.

*"It's hard for me to talk about this. See, I never had a brother, and Doc was just one year older than me. I felt very close to him. I think about it even now, so many years later. Outside of my immediate family, his*

*This photograph of Coretta Scott King ran on the cover of Life magazine on April 19, 1968. More than 30 years later, it was named one of the 50 best photographs of the second half of the twentieth century.*

was the greatest friendship I have ever known or experienced. He felt he was on earth to communicate love, period. He was, by far, the greatest man I ever met."

# CHAPTER 5

# Views of a Troubled Age

Martin Luther King, Jr., and his civil rights marchers may have brought about the most momentous social change of the 1960s, but it was not the only significant movement of the time. College students across the country presented strong opposition to the political and military establishment, with repeated protests against the war in Vietnam. There were demands for greater freedom in this country, but the United States also faced continual international instability from the Cold War with the Soviet Union and its Communist allies around the globe.

In 1962, Flip chronicled a unit of U.S. Marine special forces training for an invasion of Cuba, just 90 miles from American shores. The tense period became known as the Cuban Missile Crisis and drew the United States to the very brink of nuclear war with the Soviet Union. Three years later,

Upper left, *U.S. Marine assault team training for planned invasion of Cuba, 1962.* Right, *fighter jet firing missiles at target range near Miami.* Lower left, *U.S. Marines embarking on a troopship bound for Cuba, 1962.*

*American soldier during U.S. incursion in Dominican Republic, 1965*

Flip covered a civil war in another Caribbean trouble spot, the Dominican Republic. U.S. troops were dispatched to keep order, but they were nowhere near when Flip and a *Life* reporter were captured by rebel forces.

*"They thought we were spies with the CIA. We were lined up against the wall, and they raised their guns, and just then a lieutenant came up and yelled that we were with the Peace Corps. They let us out.*

*"That's when I realized it may be worth dying for something important, but this wasn't it. I was asked to go cover the war in Vietnam, but I said no."*

One place he did visit, repeatedly, was Berlin, the German capital city that was ground zero of the Cold War. At the end of World War II in 1945, Berlin had been divided into eastern and western sectors, with the East controlled by Communist forces and the West by the United States, Britain, and France. As more and more Germans escaped from the repression of Communist-controlled East Germany to the freedom of the West, Communist authorities built a tall, unsightly wall between the two sections of the city. It went up literally overnight, on August 13, 1961, and for 28 years served as a powerful and all too painful symbol of the ideologies that kept the world on edge.

In the first two years after the wall was built, at least 68 desperate easterners were killed as they tried to cross over to the freedom of West Berlin. Handmade memorials were left in their honor at the base of the wall on the western side. Flip returned to Berlin decade after decade, documenting the wall as it grew in size and in mythic importance.

He had made his first visit to the wall in 1962, several months after it was built. He saw the barbed-wire fences, the East German soldiers on patrol, the broken glass that had been placed on top of the wall. He saw the sad, frightened faces of children who seemed to understand that their simple games had been invaded by the politics of the Cold War.

*To give the impression of normality, East German authorities sent children to the base of the Berlin Wall to act as if they were at play, 1962.*

*A church on the eastern side of the Berlin Wall, 1962*

*East German guards on lookout*

*Glass and barbed wire at the top of the Berlin Wall*

*After East Germans jumped to freedom in the West, the windows of this building on the eastern side of the wall were bricked over. The building was later demolished.*

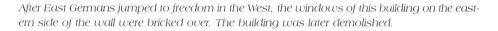

*Two views from West Berlin toward Bernauer Street in East Berlin, in 1962 (left) and 1980 (right)*

*"The thing about the Berlin Wall is that no one today knows what it looked like. It went right down the middle of a street. At first, you could look across into the windows on the other side. Then, after people jumped over the wall, they bricked over the windows."*

After the wall finally came down in 1989, inaugurating the fall of communism in Europe, Flip went back to find a changed world: East German soldiers were rolling up the barbed wire, and children were free to play without worrying about the machine guns and land mines that were arrayed along the wall to keep people from fleeing.

*"It was like New Year's Eve. Kids from all over the world were there, and people were chipping off pieces of the wall as souvenirs. I even took a few swings at it with a hammer myself. It was a huge turning point in world history, but people already seem to have forgotten about it."*

*By admitting Flip to his guard tower in March 1990, this East German soldier defied the orders of his colonel. "We don't have to listen to you anymore," he told the officer.*

*An East German soldier dismantles the electrified barbed-wire fence at the top of the Berlin Wall, 1990.*

*Two blocks from where the girl pictured on page 51 timidly played in 1962, East German children freely frolicked at the wall in 1990.*

Soon after the wall went up, President John F. Kennedy traveled to Berlin and famously announced his solidarity with the people of the divided city, declaring in German, *Ich bin ein Berliner*—"I am a Berliner." Flip had known the Kennedy clan since 1940, when he was in the same dancing class in Palm Beach with Ted Kennedy, the future senator. After John Kennedy was elected president in 1960, Flip covered him whenever he came to Florida. He photographed JFK at a football game at Miami's Orange Bowl, greeting astronauts after their return from space, and standing on the deck of a navy ship as he watched the launch of a missile from a submarine. Flip photographed the president's week-long visit to Florida in November 1963, just before he traveled on to Texas.

*President John F. Kennedy greeting John Glenn after he became the first American astronaut to orbit the earth, February 1962*

*As President Kennedy and Vice President Lyndon B. Johnson listen to scientist Wernher von Braun describe the space program, Flip can be seen directly behind the president's right shoulder. November 1963.*

*President John F. Kennedy, 1961*

*Kennedy in 1963*

*President Kennedy on the deck of a U.S. Navy ship, watching the launch of a Polaris missile from a submarine off Cape Canaveral, November 18, 1963*

*President-elect John F. Kennedy, a face in the crowd at the*
*Orange Bowl game, Miami, January 1, 1961*

*"I was with him the whole week before he died. I was riding two cars behind him in a parade in Tampa and I remember casually remarking to the other photographers, 'It seems to me that a sniper could kill the president if he wanted.' He was riding in an open car, with crowds of people on either side, and I knew how much he was hated in the South."*

On November 22, 1963, Flip was in Austin, photographing a feature on campus life at the University of Texas, when he heard that Kennedy had been shot in Dallas. He and a reporter rented a Lear jet and flew immediately to Dallas. Flip showed his *Life* magazine press pass, and a policeman escorted him into the Texas School Book Depository, a brick warehouse from which the fatal shots had been fired. The rifle of the presumed assassin, Lee Harvey Oswald, had just been taken away.

Climbing to the sixth floor, Flip took a chilling photograph of Oswald's unobstructed view of the parade route.

Book boxes were still stacked in place beneath the window. Oil was visible on the uppermost box, where Oswald had balanced his rifle. Since the police hadn't closed the road, traffic still passed on the street below. Off to the side, Flip noticed a box containing bones from Oswald's lunch of fried chicken.

*As a symbol of the nation's fallen commander-in-chief, a riderless black horse, with boots reversed in the stirrups, walked in the procession at John F. Kennedy's funeral in Washington, D.C., November 25, 1963.*

*"We were the only members of the press who got in there. You can see, as you look down at the road below, that it wasn't that difficult a shot for someone with a rifle. But, of all the photographers around, nobody else thought to go there. It's herd journalism. You should always try to get around what everyone else is doing."*

Flip was assigned by his photo agency, Black Star, to cover Kennedy's funeral in Washington. On a typical assignment, he would have as many as five cameras hanging around his neck or slung over his shoulders. Some were loaded with color film, others with black and white. In those days, color photographs were still relatively rare in magazines and were almost never seen in newspapers. It took at least an extra day to process color film, so color photos were reserved for special occasions. Nothing could be more important than the funeral of a president, and Flip was asked to shoot in color that day.

*"It was a clear, sunny day, with blue sky from one end of the horizon to the other. Everywhere you looked, there were flags and people dressed in military uniforms. There were soldiers wearing red jackets. It looked like*

*a party. It didn't look like a funeral, except for Mrs. Kennedy, who was*
*wearing the traditional widow's weeds, with a black veil.*

*"I had a really good spot, about 20 feet from Mrs. Kennedy at the*
*grave site, but I don't have a decent picture of her. It was one of the worst*
*takes I ever did. I should have switched to black and white. If I had, I*
*could have penetrated the veil because I could have overexposed the*
*film and shown her face. That's the one assignment that I still regret."*

There was one other reason why Flip wasn't able to get the pictures
that he wanted that day.

*"I was so upset and crying that I couldn't look through the viewfinder*
*and focus. I did not show at all what was distressing me so much. The*
*press is pretty hard-boiled. You have to be. You see murders; you see all*
*sorts of things. But there must have been three or four hundred writers*
*and photographers behind me. And you heard them all crying."*

———————

Flip had spent much of the 1960s on the front lines, chronicling a
decade of profound and often violent social change. He was protected
only by his camera and his wits, and in his late 30s he knew he couldn't
outrun fate forever. Two months apart in the spring of 1968, he covered
the funerals of Martin Luther King, Jr., and Robert F. Kennedy, both felled
by assassins' bullets.

*"I knew astronauts who were killed in training and I knew 19 pro-*
*fessional race-car drivers who were killed in crashes. When I covered*
*Bobby Kennedy's funeral, my third at Arlington National Cemetery, I*
*thought, I can't take this anymore. I had spent a lot of my life photo-*
*graphing news, disasters, and man's inhumanity to man. I was at a*
*stage in my life in which I would have liked to show some of the positive*
*aspects of man's relationship to man."*

———————

CHAPTER 6

# The Space Race and Beyond

Shortly after he took office in 1961, John F. Kennedy promised that the United States would have a man on the moon by the end of the decade. Today, more than 40 years after the fact, it's hard to convey the excitement of those early days when the space program was new, exciting, and daring. The first seven astronauts of the original Mercury program were nothing less than national heroes, whose every step was chronicled by a wide-eyed press.

*"These guys were superstars. We had never had anything like them before. They were all top military pilots, and everyone looked up to them. Remember, this was at the height of the Cold War, and there was a big competition with Russia to see which country would become dominant in space. Kennedy called space exploration the 'Next Frontier,' and people all over the country wanted to know what these astronauts were all about."*

*Astronaut Bruce McCandless training in a weightless underwater environment. Space Flight Center, Huntsville, Alabama, 1985.*

*McCandless with a jet-propelled backpack, training for a spacewalk. Johnson Space Center, Houston, Texas, 1983.*

*Students at NASA's Space Camp in Huntsville, Alabama, made their own rockets in the early 1980s.*

*Astronaut McCandless training with a device to capture a satellite in outer space. Denver, Colorado, 1983.*

Because *Life* magazine had an exclusive arrangement with the astronauts, Flip often photographed them at their training center at Cape Canaveral, on the eastern coast of Florida. He also chronicled their launches—still a dangerous thing in the early days of space travel—as well as the tension reflected in the faces of the astronauts' wives.

*Flip kept the camera shutter open for five seconds to capture the flight path of astronaut Gordon Cooper's Gemini spacecraft returning to earth in the dark morning sky above Houston, Texas, on August 29, 1965. Cooper's wife, Trudy, is silhouetted in the foreground. This photo won Portrait of the Year in the annual competition of the National Press Photographers Association.*

*The launch of Apollo IV, November 9, 1967*

*Inside NASA's Mission Control, 1961*

Above and right, *the first space shuttle launch from the Kennedy Space Center, April 12, 1981*

*America's first astronauts, from the Mercury program, 1961. From left, Gordon Cooper, Scott Carpenter, John Glenn, Alan Shepard, Walter Schirra, and Donald "Deke" Slayton. Not pictured, Virgil "Gus" Grissom.*

Flip was one of the few photographers admitted to NASA's secret training programs, diving into training pools with the astronauts and experiencing their weightless surroundings. On the other side of the Iron Curtain, he became the first Western photographer inside the Soviet Union's space command and training center at Star City, near Moscow.

As the 1960s wore on, Flip turned more and more toward science, exploration, and underwater photography. He occasionally teamed with Jacques Cousteau, the foremost undersea scientist and explorer of the twentieth century. Cousteau's adventures were seen in a series of popular television documentaries, and Flip portrayed Cousteau at work in the pages of *National Geographic*.

*Undersea explorer Jacques Cousteau*

*Jacques Cousteau and crew aboard research ship Calypso near Madagascar, off the south-eastern coast of Africa, 1968. Behind them is a one-person submarine used in exploration.*

*Cousteau at the controls of his one-person submarine*

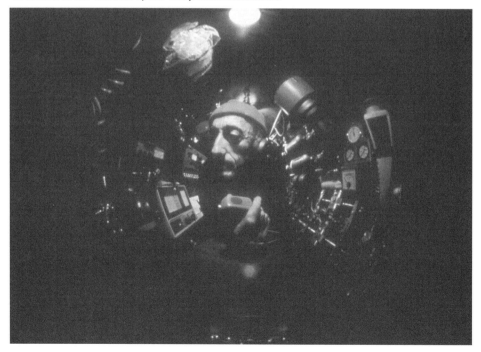

*Flip filming a documentary on the underwater Tektite habitat in the U.S. Virgin Islands, 1970*

*Flip in wet suit, 1980*

*"All my life, I've gotten bored if I shoot the same thing. I have never specialized and because of that I've been able to work for all kinds of magazines."*

Diving to the ocean floor, Flip photographed ancient shipwrecks in the Mediterranean, the North Sea, and the Caribbean. He took part in numerous underwater studies in anthropology and paleontology. He once spent a month in the Galapagos Islands off South America, photographing a scientific study. In 1970, he spent two weeks under water in the Caribbean, making a documentary film about people living in America's first non-military aquatic habitat, Tektite. In the early 1980s, when he was in his 50s, Flip photographed the discovery of the *Atocha*, a Spanish sailing ship that sank off Key West in the 1700s. Laden with gold coins and other precious cargo, the *Atocha* is the most valuable shipwreck ever discovered in American waters.

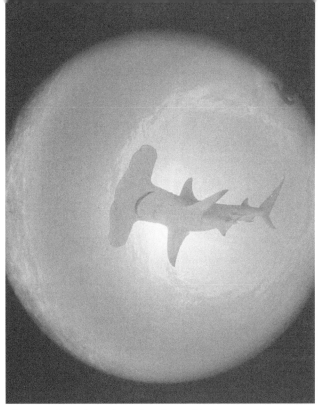

*Flip was less than three feet from this hammerhead shark when he photographed it off Grand Bahama Island. An underwater fisheye lens makes the shark appear farther away than it actually is.*

*Flip's daughter Maria swimming with a dolphin, in 1987*

*Underwater research submarine, early 1970s*

*Swimmers near Key West*

*Moray eel, near Miami*

*A 1968 Jacques Cousteau expedition to Bolivia's Lake Titicaca came up empty in its search for buried Incan treasure. Instead, Cousteau's divers discovered a previously unknown species of frog.*

*Flip's daughter Maria feeding fish, Key Largo, Florida*

*"Christ of the Abyss," an underwater sculpture in the Florida Keys*

*Blacksmith and his dog. Burnsville, North Carolina, 1956.*

*Chi Chi, the giant panda that lived at the London Zoo from
1958 to 1972. Photographed in 1969.*

*Butcher shop. Lanzarote, Canary Islands, 1968.*

*Trolley tracks leading nowhere. Berlin Wall, 1980.*

*The Arc de Triomphe at night. Paris, 1962.*

*Sunset at Stonehenge. England, 1970.*

*Iguana. Galapagos Islands, 1964.*

*Flip's daughter Maria swimming with a dolphin, 1987*

*Flip took the world's first underwater fashion photographs in 1972, off the Bahama Islands.*

*Divers salvaging an ancient amphora, or strorage jug, from a 2,000-year-old shipwreck off Bodrum, Turkey, 1967*

*Drew Barrymore. Los Angeles, 2002.*

*Mayor of a Bolivian town, 1969*

Left, *Coins from a Dutch shipwreck in the Shetland Islands off the coast of Scotland, 1968*

Right, *An astronaut trains underwater at Johnson Space Center, Houston, Texas.*

*Snoop Dogg. Photographed by Flip's stepson Joe Toreno.*

*Fashion photograph by Joe Toreno's partner, Amanda Friedman*

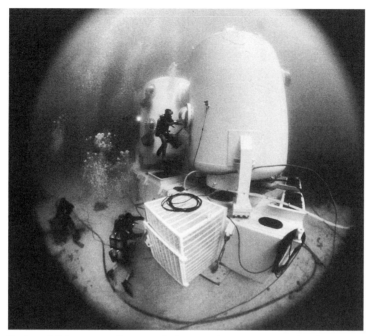

*Project Tektite, an underwater habitat in the U.S. Virgin Islands, 1970*

*Clay amphoras from a shipwreck near Bodrum, Turkey, 1967*

*Underwater exploratory vessel, 1980s*

*Blacktip shark, Bahamas*

*Silver pieces of eight from a Spanish shipwreck of the 1620s, discovered in the Bahamas, 1971*

*Iguanas on the Galapagos Islands, off the west coast of Ecuador, 1964*

*Images from the Galapagos Islands*

*Tortoise, Galapagos Islands*

*Sea lions, Galapagos Islands*

The underwater cameras and equipment that Flip began working with in the late 1950s proved to have an unexpected benefit: they were perfect for photographing hurricanes. The first time one of Flip's pictures was featured on the cover of *Life* was in 1961, when he photographed a hurricane coming ashore in Texas. Outdoing himself a couple of years later, he had a reporter tie him to a light pole as a hurricane roared through Miami.

*"I wasn't out there that long—I'm not that foolish. I stayed there just long enough to get my pictures."*

*This photograph of Hurricane Carla bearing down on Galveston, Texas, was Flip's first cover shot for Life magazine, September 22, 1961.*

*Flip tied himself to a utility pole to photograph Hurricane Betsy as it came ashore in Miami, September 8, 1965. During the next hurricane, the light poles were snapped off.*

*Aftermath of Hurricane Carla, Galveston, Texas, 1961*

Flip's underwater shots were his most technically difficult assignments. Instead of using flash, Flip usually illuminated his underwater shots with

a 1,000-watt floodlight attached by a 300-foot cable to a generator in a boat. An assistant held the light while Flip, wearing a wet suit, air tanks, and scuba mask, swam around looking for the best angle. Still, in everything he covered, no matter how technically complex, Flip was always more interested in the people who made the stories than in the razzle-dazzle of futuristic equipment.

*"As technically demanding as my underwater shots were, it was more difficult to talk people into letting me cover things. It takes a lot of psychol-ogy and human understanding, plus the ability to talk their language. That was true not just of the civil rights movement but of racecar drivers."*

From civil rights to astronauts, Flip was always drawn to the triumph of the human spirit. Similarly, in photographing car races in the United States and Europe, he found the personalities behind the wheel more compelling than the gears and grease of racing.

*"I didn't care at all about the cars and the crashes. I was much more interested in the drivers, the mechanics, the behind-the-scenes stuff. I pio-neered this way of really concentrating on the drivers, not the car. In Europe, I often crouched on the painted line at the edge of the track. The cars would brush me, literally. But I got incredible pictures. I finally stopped doing it when Bruce McLaren told me, 'Either you'll kill me, or I'll kill you.'"*

Dan Gurney celebrating his victory with A. J. Foyt as the first American driving team to win the 24 Hours of Le Mans race, 1967

Dan Gurney at the Indianapolis 500, 1963

*After running out of gas on the final lap, Australian driver Jack Brabham pushes his car across the finish line at Sebring, Florida, in 1959. By completing the race, he won the world Grand Prix driving championship.*

*Belgian driver Olivier Gendebien winning the 12 Hours of Sebring race, 1959*

*Engine and wheel of Jim Hall's Chaparral racecar, 1966*

*The start of the 12 Hours of Sebring race, 1963*

A few years later, McLaren became one of the 19 drivers Flip knew who died in crashes. Having seen so much danger and sorrow on land, Flip increasingly found serenity in his work under water. In 1966, in the waters of Puget Sound, near Seattle, he became the first photographer to swim with a killer whale, named Namu. Even then, he didn't feel fear so much as a sense of joy at being alone in nature with a magnificent animal.

*Namu, the first killer whale photographed under water in open seas. Puget Sound, Washington, 1966.*

"People always ask, 'What was your most interesting and exciting assignment?' It was Namu. There is no getting around it, out of everything I've done.

"My idea was to lie down at the bottom of the lake and look straight up to get a silhouette. I got these beautiful bubbles coming out of the top of his head because he was exhaling. Every time he exhaled, he squeaked. Whenever I made a squeaking sound, he would squeak back.

"I had a sense of doing something no one else had done before, of being alone with this wonderful creature that was like a big St. Bernard, a really friendly dog. You could hold on to his fin and take a ride. He'd dip down in the water and let you get on his back.

"I can remember every minute when I was shooting. Everything was so exciting and so much fun. The King pictures were more serious. But this was something that was just a joy."

# CHAPTER 7

# A Life in Pictures

Flip Schulke has been a photojournalist for more than half a century and has worked for the leading magazines of his time, including the legendary *Life*. Until it folded in 1972, *Life* was the most popular weekly magazine in the country, with as many as 10 million subscribers. It was a combination of *People, Time,* and *Sports Illustrated.* No magazine since has been able to take its place.

Flip has spent his entire career as a freelance photographer, or someone who signs on for particular jobs with different publications but ultimately remains his own boss. It's a hard way to make a living because when you're not on assignment, you don't get paid. It has meant that Flip has had to build his reputation one story at a time, one image at a time.

Despite being asked more than once, he never joined the staff of *Life* or any other magazine or newspaper because, under copyright laws, the publisher would have owned all rights to his pictures. By remaining a freelance, Flip has retained ownership of all his photographs and their copyrights.

*"One of the good things about being a freelance is that you have a lot of freedom. I could suggest ideas to different magazines, but I could also turn down things I wasn't interested in by saying I had another assignment, which you can't do if you're on a staff.*

*"The main reason I refused to work on the staff of* Life *magazine is because all my original pictures and copyrights would have belonged to* Life. *I felt that what I was doing was important and I wanted to hold on to it. When I was covering civil rights, I knew that I was photographing history."*

As a result, Flip retains ownership of every one of the 500,000 pictures he has shot in his career, including more than 11,000 images documenting Martin Luther King, Jr., and the civil rights movement—the largest private collection in the world.

From his earliest days in Minnesota, when he was photographing weddings and town parades, Flip learned the many technical details that go into getting a picture right: lighting, film speeds, composition, and simply knowing where to stand. Over the years, he has used at least 75 cameras in his work. Most of his photos for *Life* were taken with Nikon cameras, but he has also used Pentax, Canon, Rollei-flex, and other brands. He has shot thousands of images on both black-and-white and color film but has a lingering preference for black and white.

*"The biggest difference between color and black and white is the separation of colors. When you're shooting black and white, you have to get contrasts, or else everything will look gray. I pushed the limits of black and white and I was looking for things with dramatic impact, with a lot of contrast.*

*"I think if you talk to any photographer my age, they'll say they prefer black and white. There are still occasions where you'll be able to tell the story and convey your feelings about what's happening better by getting*

*rid of the color. Today, the major magazines are going back to black and white. We have so much color around us, in magazines, advertising, and television, that whenever you want to make something stand out, you run it in black and white."*

The eye for photography is not easily explained. Many people can master its technical complexities, but only the rare photographer has the gift to infuse his or her pictures with the light and life that raise them to the level of art. When dozens of cameras focus on the same scene, how does one photographer consistently get the best shots? These are some of the lessons that Flip is now passing on to younger generations.

*"People always ask, 'How do you know when to take the picture?' The only way I can explain it is when it feels right. Always trust your gut instinct. A good picture is luck, a lot of times. But you have to be prepared for it. You make your own luck."*

For Flip, that preparation has always begun with an insatiable curiosity and an appetite for learning. When talking to students, he emphasizes that a photojournalist's most important tool is not necessarily his camera but an awareness of a larger world beyond the lens. He recommends that prospective students acquire a wider perspective on life by studying sociology, psychology, and, above all, history. Acknowledging both his professional achievements and his long involvement with education, Rider University in Lawrenceville, New Jersey, awarded Flip an honorary doctor of laws degree in 2003.

*"In today's world, an aspiring photojournalist has to go to college. We learn from the past. There's no other way. You must constantly read—news-papers, magazines, and books—and follow the news on television. You don't stop learning when you leave the university. That's just a beginning.*

*"Photojournalism is a combination of art and journalism—it's documentation in an artistic way. It's no different from what a good writer does. What I want to do now is pass this on, to be able to inspire young people to go into journalism."*

Flip is often asked about his experiences with Martin Luther King, Jr., and about the glory years of *Life*, but he doesn't want anyone to think that the best days of photojournalism are over. The large-format weekly picture magazines may be gone, but there are still ample opportunities for photojournalists to do significant work.

*"Just because* Life *and* Look *folded, it doesn't mean photojournalism is dead, despite what some of the old photographers might say. Go to the newsstand, and you'll see hundreds of magazines and other venues for photojournalists today. I never specialized and because of that I was able to work for all kinds of magazines. It's the same today.*

*"One thing you have to remember—and it was true throughout my career—is that the really big stories don't come along that often. The majority of all assignments are not exciting, and they're not dull: they're what I call bread-and-butter assignments.*

*"Young photographers can make it today through their own drive, reading, watching the news, and making judicious—I emphasize the word 'judicious'—use of the Internet. If you try, it's amazing how many things you can do. The best example I know is my own stepson, Joe Toreno, and his partner, Amanda Friedman."*

Joe is the son of Flip's wife, Donna, whom he married in 1991. After becoming interested in photography in high school, Joe went to the Rochester Institute of Technology in upstate New York, where he met Amanda. Instead of following the common path to New York City, where they would likely have spent years as assistants to photographers with bigger names, Joe and Amanda moved to Los Angeles and launched freelance careers. By their mid-20s, their work was being featured regularly in *Time, Newsweek, U.S. News & World Report, Interview,* and *Wired* magazines.

*"I use them as examples because no one knows Joe is my stepson. He and Amanda have done it all on their own. I have never called anyone to get them work. I mention them because there are still a lot of possibilities in this field. Photojournalism is like all creative fields—there's a pyramid of achievement, and there's no stopping someone who wants to reach the top.*

*"The joy a photojournalist gets out of his work must be in the act of taking the photograph, solving the problem of the moment. You have to take pride in the actual picture when you're shooting it. To do this, you must be aware of everything around you; you must keep educating yourself as widely as possible; you must come up with ideas; you must keep abreast of the current market; you must keep well grounded in current techniques.*

*"My biggest problem with young photographers is that they don't think about context. They think about drama. You've got to know where to point your camera.*

*"I would also advise young people that their appearance matters. Photojournalists have a bad reputation for looking and acting like slobs. If you're out on assignment, meeting important people, you should dress up and look respectable. It will open a lot of doors for you."*

At some fundamental level, every journalist is idealistic about the world and wants to bring about change. An old adage that the profession should "comfort the afflicted and afflict the comfortable" is as true now as ever. Journalists are often accused of showing bias in how they present the news, but Flip has never seen this as a problem. In fact, he thinks there is something false about trying to maintain strict neutrality on important moral issues.

*"Journalism schools try to teach their students to be 'unbiased.' They should use the word 'fair,' because most people know what it means to be fair.*

*"About certain things in life, you have to be an advocate. You can't just present two sides of a story and try to be as balanced as you can. I've yet to see a situation where there are good intellectual and emotional arguments that are almost exactly the same for both sides. My point is that, with some things, there isn't another side. For example, there are not two ways to look at segregation.*

*"It all relates back to the unfair things I had seen throughout my life and the unfair treatment I felt I had from my father. Some people believe in getting even. I don't believe in that. I believe in 'Don't get mad—expose it.'"*

More than 30 years after Flip's first cover for *Life* magazine, of a hurricane blowing ashore in Texas, he had another first-hand experience with a hurricane. His house was in the direct path of Hurricane Andrew, which ravaged parts of Miami in 1992. He was inside as the roof was torn off by winds estimated at 155 miles per hour. Much of his furniture and equipment was destroyed, but he managed to save nearly all of his photographic negatives, including his civil rights collection, by putting them in trash bags before the storm hit. He later moved 75 miles up the coast to West Palm Beach, where he maintains his office.

His archives of over 800,000 photographs, which he salvaged from the storm, will be housed in the Center for American History at the University of Texas at Austin. More than 9,000 of Flip's images have been digitally converted to Kodak CD-ROM interactive discs and will be available for study online, to inspire future photojournalists and to serve as a lasting testament to the dramatic times in which he lived.

*"A photograph fills different needs, at different times in life. There are ideas and understandings that people can never fully experience without photography. It's not merely the camera you are focusing—you are*

*Flip standing in the ruins of his Miami house after it was destroyed by Hurricane Andrew, August 24, 1992. Photo by Gary Truman.*

*focusing yourself. Then, when you touch the button, what is inside of you comes out. It's the most basic form of creativity. Part of you is now permanent."*

Proving that his eye is still as sharp as ever, Flip was back on the job at age 72 in 2002, photographing the assembled skeleton of a prehistoric mammoth in a Florida museum. He had first documented the mammoth 34 years earlier, diving underwater to photograph the bones as they were unearthed from the bottom of a river.

*"Once I was out there shooting, everything came back—the joy, the high of it. It was just like the old days. I want to communicate life as I see it. I'm still a journalist, and I still think journalism is the highest calling in photography."*

*"Photography can make a person pause in his rush through life. Photography can teach people to look, to feel, to remember, in a way that they didn't know they could.*

*"When I look at one of my own pictures, it all comes back to me. I can look back on my life, and there isn't anything I would change."*

On assignment for National Geographic in 1968, Flip chronicled the unearthing of the bones of a prehistoric mammoth from the Aucilla River in northern Florida. Below, scientists examine the mammoth's enormous bones and teeth. Facing page: Thirty-four years later in June 2002, Flip photographed the skeleton as it was assembled in the Florida Museum of Natural History in Gainesville, making it his longest story ever. Photo by Gary Truman.

## BOOKS BY FLIP SCHULKE

*Underwater Photography for Everyone.* Saddle River, N.J.: Prentice-Hall, 1976.

*Martin Luther King, Jr.: A Documentary, Montgomery to Memphis.* New York: Norton, 1976.

*King Remembered,* with Penelope McPhee. New York: Norton, 1976.

*Fotografen und Filmen für Taucher,* with Albert Mueller. Zurich: Ruschilkon, 1982.

*Your Future in Space,* with Penelope McPhee. New York: Crown, 1986.

*He Had a Dream: Martin Luther King, Jr., and the Civil Rights Movement.* New York: Norton, 1995.

*Muhammad Ali: The Birth of a Legend, Miami 1961–1964,* with Matt Schudel. New York: St. Martin's, 1999.

See also

*Flip Schulke Archives: www.flipschulke.com.*

*Peter Fetterman Gallery, Santa Monica, CA: www.peterfetterman.com.*

# INDEX